You & Your Family

Adapted From Material Written By

**Robert Brent • Jim Rovira
Louis T. Smith • Gary Speer
Larry Thomas**

Radiant Life

1445 Boonville Avenue
Springfield, Missouri 65802–1894
02-0152

National Director: Arlyn R. Pember
Editor in Chief: Michael H. Clarensau
Adult Editor: Paul W. Smith
Series Coordinator: Aaron D. Morgan
Design/Cover Illustration: Jared Van Bruaene

Printed in the United States of America

ISBN 0–88243–152–8

The leader guide for this book can be ordered from Gospel Publishing
House (02–0252) at 1–800–641–4310.

Contents

Preface

You & Your Family, one of four books in the *Biblical Living Series*, will assist you in strengthening and deepening your relationships with your parents, as well as any siblings, spouse, or children you might have. Each chapter will help you evaluate relevant Bible passages by asking you thought-provoking questions, many of which call on you to make application to your personal life.

You can read *You & Your Family* on its own or as a part of the *Biblical Living Series*. It is recommended that you read only one chapter a week so you can allow each chapter's biblical truths and instructions time to "sink in." Some of the questions will require ongoing action on your part; do not neglect these if you want to get the full benefit from this book.

If you are reading *You & Your Family* as part of a small group or Sunday School class, be sure to complete the assigned chapter before each meeting. The discussions, work sheets, and activities in which you will participate during your group's next meeting will be most beneficial if you have read and filled out the chapter being covered.

This preface would not be complete without recognizing the authors whose studies for Radiant Life's young adult and adult dated curriculum were adapted for this book. Larry Thomas is both a pastor and the Sunday School Training Coordinator for the Assemblies of God. Gary Speer is a freelance writer. Both Robert Brent and Louis T. Smith pastor congregations.

Aaron Morgan
Biblical Living Series Coordinator
Springfield, Missouri

Part One

Loving Your Family Members

If you were fortunate to live in a loving home when you were a young child, you probably thought your family was concerned mainly with meeting all your needs. As you grew older, however, you realized that your relationships with these people involved responsibility on your part as well.

Your responsibilities to your family do not disappear with time or distance. A give-and-take approach to family living continues to develop as family members mature. If you are wise, you will try to maintain a good relationship with your family all your life, looking for ways to benefit from this interaction and contribute to your family members' lives.

This unit will look at the family from several different angles, each centering on a particular type of relationship, but all of them pointing to the need for godly love and understanding within any family group. Getting along with everyone in your family may be a challenge, but it is a rewarding one.

Learning From Your Parents

1–1. How do you think you would be different, both positively and negatively, if you had been raised by people other than your parents?

Whether or not you would like to admit it, your parents had, and continue to have, an enormous influence on who you are. Other factors, both internal and external, have had much effect on you today. But the influence your parents had on the development of your personality and thinking during your childhood and young adulthood will continue throughout your life.

Parental influence can be either positive or negative. As in all of life, if you follow God's plan, even negative experiences can have positive results. This chapter observes how different people in the Bible related to their parents. Their examples can serve to help you draw closer to your parents and benefit from their wisdom and experience.

Honoring Parents

The Bible gives you timeless principles for honoring your parents. God placed such an emphasis on honoring parents that He specifically commanded children to do so in the Ten Commandments. "Honor your father and your mother," the fifth commandment states, "so that you may live long in the land the Lord your God is giving you" (Exodus 20:12).

1–2. What do you think it means to "honor" your parents?

1–3. How good were you as a child at honoring your parents? Explain how well or poorly you honor them now that you are an adult.

God's command to the Israelites to honor their parents carried a great blessing that went beyond individual benefit to national impact. God told the young nation of Israel that if parents were shown respect and honor, they would enjoy longevity in the land of blessing they were destined to enter. The health and longevity of their society depended, at least in part, on how well succeeding generations of Israelites did at honoring their parents.

It is probably significant that the command to honor parents was the first of the Ten Commandments dealing with interpersonal relationships in the community. You learn to respect others by respecting your parents, the first important people in your life.

1–4. *Did the Israelites continue to honor their parents through the following generations? What was the result? Is there a parallel to today's society?*

You can look at society today and see how a lack of respect for parents has had far-reaching effects. In more and more homes, children are growing up without learning to respect parental authority. This generation in turn moves into life unable to respect other authorities as well.

The wise Solomon repeatedly encouraged the honoring of one's parents in such passages as Proverbs 1:8,9; 3:1,2; and 23:22–25 by pointing out the benefits of taking their advice to heart.

1–5.   *Name several things you learned from your parents that have blessed your adult life. How have you honored them for the good things they taught you as a child?*

In Genesis 47:5–10, you can see Joseph's clear example of honoring a parent. Think how easy it would be for someone with power and influence like Joseph to let go of a valuable relationship with a parent. Joseph was a ruler whose influence spread from Egypt to surrounding nations during a famine. Yet in these verses his respect and personal regard for his father Jacob, a mere nomadic shepherd in the eyes of Joseph's Egyptian peers, is evident. It does not matter how successful or self-reliant you may become; you can still benefit from the an honoring relationship with godly parents.

1–6.   *Does God expect you to honor your parents even if they are ungodly or do not seem worthy of respect? Explain your answer.*

Returning Care

Sometimes, you are called on to give back to your parents more than honor. Advances in medicine and health services have made it possible for people to live longer. But longer life spans, while wonderful opportunities to extend meaningful relationships into third and possibly fourth generations, often raise difficult questions about practical care for parents who can no longer adequately care for themselves.

If you have had to take care of a parent due to illness or infirmity, you know that assisting an aging parent can be a stressful time for both you and your family. Additionally, the reversal of roles, in which you look after the person who used to look after you, can be as emotionally traumatic for your parent as it is for you. But if you have a healthy relationship with your parents, you will find the strength and wisdom you need to return care to one or both of them.

1–7.   *Have you or someone you know had a parent live in your home? How did you cope with this arrangement? What did you gain from your parent's living with you?*

Again, Joseph is a good example for you to follow. Genesis 45:23–28 describes how he sent Jacob all the provisions he needed for a comfortable and safe journey to Egypt. There Joseph would provide a comfortable place for his father and the rest of his family to live in peace. With Egypt's wealth at his disposal, Joseph was able to provide lavishly for the care of his elderly parent, settling him in one of the country's most fertile regions, Goshen.

This account demonstrates one way for children to return care to their parents. Before coming to Egypt, Jacob had been enduring the famine that had depleted the resources of that region. Joseph's assistance to his aging father bountifully met some critical material needs.

Joseph's unique position does bring up an important point. Not everyone can have the finest care available. For many adult children of aging parents, cost is a major factor in choosing whether a nursing home, a retirement community, an assisted living apartment, or home health care is the best option. It is vital that everyone involved recognizes that what is most important is not that the parents live in the best style, but that their needs—physical, social, emotional, and spiritual—are adequately met.

1–8.   What, in your opinion, must be the main priority for believers who truly honor their parents when making decisions about providing care?

Jesus himself is an example of returning care to parents. As the weight of sin crushed Jesus and as death closed in, He made certain His widowed mother was cared for by placing her in the hands of John, one of His most trusted disciples (John 19:26,27). Allow Jesus' selfless action to inspire you to consider the needs of your aging parents even in the middle of your own life struggles and hectic schedule.

Listening To Counsel

Earlier in this chapter, you were encouraged to honor your parents for the things they have taught you. Living by the principles you learned from your parents is a wonderful and practical way to give them honor. You can also honor them by seeking and listening to their advice in specific situations.

Many people have little patience for the advice of older generations, relying exclusively on the counsel of their peers. As a result, they make many costly mistakes they could have avoided. If you do not want to live your life by trial and error, heed the wisdom your parents have gained through a lifetime of experience.

1–9. *Does asking for your parents' advice mean you must always do what they advise? How can you make sure your parents know you honor them even when you do not follow their advice?*

Of course, the greatest advice any parent can give you is to follow God. King David based his advice to Solomon on this principle. In verses 9 and 20 of 1 Chronicles 28, David made it clear to Solomon that his greatest source of guidance would be God. During the early years of his reign, Solomon had the foresight to follow his father's advice. Because he did, the Lord gave him the wonderful gift of wisdom, making Solomon the wisest man ever to live. Because he could listen to an earthly father who instructed him to seek God, he could listen in turn to God, who gave him wisdom beyond compare. It pays to listen, learn, and seek counsel from your parents.

In 1 Kings 2:1–4, you can see each generation that learns to reap the wisdom of parents can have a dramatic impact on succeeding generations as well. David made it clear to his son that God's blessings to their family line depended on each generation's obedience to God.

Chapter Review

Before ending this chapter, it must be mentioned that some adults have great difficulty in honoring their parents. Due to tragic experiences, their relationships with their parents are strained or even destroyed. The negative influence of an ungodly parent can be lifelong as well. That influence can even make it difficult for some children to accept God as their Heavenly Father.

If life with your parents has been marked by discord, you may feel it is impossible to rebuild that relationship. Remember that God is able to develop in you a love for your parents that you could not develop on your own. He can give you the wisdom you need to communicate His love and compassion toward them.

If you grew up with godly parents, take some time to thank God for the blessing that experience has been in your life. Ask yourself if you are taking advantage of opportunities for continued involvement with your parents. The benefits you can receive throughout life are immeasurable.

Valuing Your
Grandparents' Legacy

Like many people, you probably have happy childhood memories of times spent with your grandparents—vacations at their home, holidays, special treats from the kitchen, and of course those sly little smiles and winks when they indulged you in some way your parents might not have done. But grandparents are more than kind people who provide you with special childhood memories. They can play an active role in your development, both socially and spiritually. Especially now that you are an adult, you can benefit from their valuable counsel and guidance.

This chapter will encourage you to cultivate a deeper, more mature relationship with these wonderful people. And if your grandparents are no longer living, it may prod you to initiate close relationships with other elderly people.

Facing Aging With Them

Most likely, your grandparents helped you face the timeless struggles of the elementary and teen years—skinned knees, lost pets, first dates, broken hearts. Shared memories of their

you know that others before you survived
times frightening years.

When you were growing up, how did your grandparents help you understand and cope with life?

Now that you are an adult and your grandparents are aging, who is there to encourage them through these sometimes frightening years? Unlike some societies, ours does not revere the elderly. Your grandparents have probably retired from the workforce and may need ongoing medical care, making them less valuable to a society that measures a person's worth by what he or she produces minus what he or she consumes. They may be feeling the loss of their perceived usefulness.

2–2.   *How have your grandparents handled the realities of aging?*

2-3. *What practical things can you do to help your grandparents as they grow older and less able to do things on their own?*

What is your role in helping your grandparents face old age with dignity and strength? Obviously, you cannot offer advice from your own experience: nothing you have faced is quite like coming face-to-face with your mortality. You can, however, remind them of the great respect the Bible shows the elderly.

2-4. *Read Job 12:12; Proverbs 16:31; and 20:29. What can you do this week to make your grandparents feel valued for their wisdom and experience?*

Knowing you are interested in what they have to say on a variety of topics reaffirms to your grandparents that they are needed by others. They are also encouraged by knowing they are still important to God. Isaiah 46:4 was spoken to the entire nation of Israel, but it is true for all believing seniors: "Even to your old age and gray hairs I am he, I am he who will sustain you." Your grandparents may be discouraged because they cannot do as much for themselves and others as they once could. But you can remind them that God will see to it that their needs will be met.

Respecting Your Elders

Because you are a product of a youth-oriented society, it may be necessary to review the importance of respecting the elderly. God himself commanded it in Leviticus 19:32: "Rise in the presence of the aged, show respect for the elderly and revere your God. I am the Lord."

2–5. *Why do you think respect for your elders and reverence for God are included in one command? What are the implications of your answer?*

Why does God place such stock in respecting the elderly? One reason could be their ability to guide young persons in making decisions. This is negatively illustrated in 1 Kings 12:6–15. Because Solomon's son Rehoboam followed the hotheaded advice of his peers instead of the experienced voices of his father's advisors, he lost half his kingdom. Your elders may not always be correct, but they are usually at least partially correct.

One pastor expressed appreciation for the older members of his congregation for providing a balancing perspective. Experience made their prayer lives more effective. And their wisdom was a resource in difficult situations. He would often go to them and seek counsel, knowing they would be in prayer with him about all situations.

2–6. *How have you benefited from your grandparents' advice? Do you think respect is a fair exchange for getting to learn from their experience?*

Of course, you will have times when you simply do not agree with your grandparents. While they are not as ignorant of current trends as you may think, your grandparents are from a completely different era and likely have a greatly different perspective on many issues. At such times, remember to show proper respect: they probably know some things you do not. As Paul advised one young pastor: "Do not rebuke an older man harshly" (1 Timothy 5:1).

2–7. *How have you handled disagreements between you and your grandparents? Do you find it easy or difficult in such situations to maintain a respectful attitude?*

Receiving A Spiritual Heritage

If you are careful to maintain a good relationship with your grandparents, you may reap one of the greatest benefits you can in life—a spiritual heritage. Your grandparents are the main connection to your family's past, including its spiritual traditions. And they can be a wonderful source of direction for you as you build on those traditions with your family.

Admittedly, your family may have little spirituality in its recent past. Your grandparents may not be believers or may have only accepted Christ recently. But you can still learn a great deal from them that will help you grow in your faith. You may come to understand what shaped the morals and philosophy of life you grew up with in your family.

2–8.   What is your family's spiritual heritage? Is it Catholic or Protestant? mainline or Pentecostal? multi-generational or a recent religious interest?

2–9.   How can your grandparents help you learn more about your family history, especially its religious history?

Genesis 48:1–20 is the account of Jacob's passing on his blessing to his grandsons, Ephraim and Manasseh, before his death. Jacob's blessing was not a quickly muttered, "Go with God." He very deliberately allowed insight to guide words of blessing that would shape his grandson's futures. He was showing them their place in the family's spiritual heritage.

2–10. How have you seen your grandparents' influence in your Christian walk?

You can also learn a great deal from your grandparents' personal relationship with the Lord. After years of knowing and living for Jesus, your grandparents probably have a big-picture perspective of how God interacts with His people. One aged believer expressed it well: "I was young and now I am old, yet I have never seen the righteous forsaken" (Psalm 37:25).

2–11. What have you learned from your grandparents about being a Christian?

Psalm 71:17,18 exemplifies the yearning of many older believers to see their faith passed on to the young. If your grandparents are Christians, they are undoubtedly interested in sharing the secrets of successful, godly living with you that have taken them a lifetime to learn. Even non-believing grandparents want you to heed the moral life lessons they have taught you.

2–12. How might you "draw out" the spiritual wisdom your grandparents have gained in their walk with God?

Chapter Review

Instead of going along with society's relatively low view of the elderly, take the lead in giving your own grandparents the honor that God says they deserve. As with all family relationships, there may have been some difficulties. But the fact remains your grandparents deserve your utmost respect, even if solely for their being your elders. Be humble enough to listen to them with an open heart.

What if your grandparents are no longer living? Consider "adopting" an older believer as your unofficial grandparent. Spend time with him or her. Listen. Learn. And pray that God will use your relationship to bless both you and this spiritual grandparent.

Getting Along With Your Siblings

This chapter will help you look at an essential area for successful family relationships—sibling harmony. The Psalmist expressed the joy of the ideal sibling relationship: "How good and how pleasant when brothers live together in unity!" (Psalm 133:1). A happy, harmonious home is one in which the children grow up contributing to each other's development.

Anyone raised with siblings knows this condition is not automatic. In fact, the first human conflict recorded in the Bible was due to sibling rivalry. This chapter will give you three fundamental steps for developing and maintaining harmony with your brothers and sisters.

Recognizing Individuality

If you want to get along with your siblings, you must respect each of them for the person he or she is. Every child that is born into a family is different. Each is an individual with his or her own likes, dislikes, and preferences for what he or she considers important.

Jacob and Esau illustrate just how different even twins can be. According to Genesis 25:21–27, the differences in their appearance, interests, and temperaments began early and became more distinct as they grew from boys to men. Sadly, neither the twins nor their parents seem to have respected these differences, making the family ripe for conflict.

3–1.   Briefly describe yourself and each of your siblings.

3–2.   What aspects of your siblings' personalities do you find most difficult to accept?

It was probably easy for you to make such a list. You are undoubtedly well aware of the things you consider to be your siblings' "faults." This is most likely because you, like almost everyone else, view your own habits and personality traits as the "norm." If you want to have a good relationship with your siblings, however, you must also examine yourself by what your siblings think about you.

3–3. *What faults do you think your siblings would say you have?*

3–4. *How did the previous question make you reconsider what is truly a fault and what is simply a difference? What one thing about each sibling can you accept as a difference and not a fault?*

To provide the best environment for peace among your siblings, you must also acknowledge that each one's personal makeup will result in differing priorities. For example, Mary and Martha's different priorities come across in Luke 10:38–40. During one of Jesus' visits to their home, Martha concentrated on hospitality duties while Mary contentedly sat in on Jesus' conversation with the disciples and Lazarus. Neither sister would have been wrong except that Martha became angry that Mary did not place as much importance in playing the hostess as she did. Jesus corrected Martha, not for her personal priorities, but for her intolerance of Mary's priorities.

3–5.   *How do you and your siblings' priorities differ? What can you learn from the things your siblings consider important?*

Settling Disputes

Unless there is mutual respect for each other's individuality, conflict is inevitable. Jacob, his mother's favorite, used Esau's hunger after a hunt to gain the birthright (Genesis 25:29–34). The incident reflects a lifetime of uneasy coexistence between the two opposites. This undercurrent of resentment finally erupted when the twins were middle-aged and the crafty Jacob tricked their elderly father into giving him the blessing that was rightfully Esau's (Genesis 27). It was the final straw for Esau, who swore he would finally kill his hated twin. Instead of repenting of his deception, Jacob ran away. Because of one conflict, the twins did not see each other for the next 20 years.

3–6.   *What major conflict have you had with a sibling? How did the two of you handle your dispute?*

Nothing is told of what happened to Esau during the 20-year period, but Jacob found himself being the one deceived and manipulated. His experiences changed him, until he felt he had to at least try to be reconciled with his brother. Take a few moments to read the account in Genesis 32:3–21.

Learning Esau was on his way, Jacob developed an elaborate plan to ease his brother's temper. You could say that once again Jacob was trying to manipulate the situation to avoid being harmed. But the point is that a humbled Jacob was willing to do whatever was necessary to restore the broken relationship.

3–7. *How could you take the first step in solving a disagreement between you and a sibling?*

Also note that Jacob made this problem a matter of prayer (verses 9–12). He knew that, ultimately, reconciliation with Esau depended on God's intervention. Thankfully, God takes joy in mediating between people. It is what He did for Mary and Martha in their dispute (Luke 10:41,42) and what He wants to do for you and your siblings when you disagree.

3–8. *Write a brief prayer asking for God's help in making things right between you and a sibling.*

If the rift between you and your sibling is severe, you may need to enlist the help of others—mutual friends, parents, a pastor, or even a Christian counselor. Objective mediators can offer invaluable assistance in getting you and your sibling to look beyond your own feelings.

3–9. **List several people you and your siblings trust and respect who could help settle a major dispute.**

Whatever you can do to mend a torn relationship with a sibling, consider doing it. Trust God to give you the wisdom to bring about the reconciliation that is pleasing to Him.

Growing Closer

Ideally, a family should grow closer as it members grow older and mature. Doing this, however, requires breaking down some of the barriers that may have been erected earlier in life. The rift between Esau and Jacob had affected all of their family for two decades. Now it was nearing an end. Read the account of this reunion in Genesis 33:1–11.

Jacob offered no small demonstration of his humility. He made the first move, sending gifts ahead of him and bowing before Esau seven times. These actions were important for Jacob, but his once-angry brother did not need them to spur him to forgiveness. Esau's welcoming kiss and hugs showed that he had already forgiven his brother.

3–10. What have you been holding against a sibling that you need to forgive him or her for even if he or she does not make the first move?

Sadly, Jacob and Esau went their separate ways after this brief meeting (Genesis 33:12–17). They were officially restored, but they had no relationship to build on.

Such life-long enmity between brothers is not the norm. You probably have relationships with your siblings that are reasonably close. And with a little effort on your part, those relationships can be even closer.

3–11. What can you do to initiate a closer relationship with each of your siblings?

Life is too difficult for you to face without the mutual support of your siblings. Use the peaceful times to do all you can to strengthen your relationships with your brothers and sisters. Then, when one of you faces a trial, the others can offer loving support that is well received.

Chapter Review

You and your siblings probably squabbled a lot as children, which is very common. But if you are still fighting now that you are adults, you are missing out on a mature relationship of mutual consideration, respect, and reliability. Learn from the mistakes of Jacob and Esau. Deal quickly with arguments with your siblings, come to an agreement, and do all you can to keep your relationships current and close. You can change your friends, but your siblings will always remain.

3–12. How have you been inspired by this passage to improve your relationship with one or more of your siblings?

God can help you with extended family relationships.

Improving Your Relative Relationships

Cousins, uncles, aunts, nephews, nieces, and in-laws all add their individual, if indirect, influences to a family. This influence is often positive, but there are sad exceptions. You must show love to every person God has placed in your family. Through contrast and comparison, this chapter will use biblical examples to illustrate some of the keys to forming a positive, extended family structure.

Cousins

4–1. *Briefly describe your cousins and the kind of relationship you have with each of them.*

In Genesis 21:1–10, Abraham's family split into two branches when he sent Hagar and Ishmael their way. Isaac was the son of promise; conflict with his half brother Ishmael had to be avoided. As part of God's promise to Abraham regarding all his descendants, Ishmael was also blessed and became a nation.

Years later, Joseph, a descendant of Abraham through Isaac, had an unpleasant encounter with a band of traders descended through Ishmael (Genesis 37:25–28,36). Joseph was sold to these distant cousins by his own brothers. The Ishmaelites, in turn, took the young man to Egypt, where they sold him in the slave market.

You would probably never consider selling one of your cousins into slavery (at least not seriously), but you may find it easy to forget the family ties that you have with them. Most people are in fairly regular contact with their cousins during childhood, but they often lose track of each other when they become adults. This may have easily happened to you.

4–2. *What things have distanced you from your cousins? If you have grown apart, how could you renew a closer relationship?*

Of course, it may be that you and your cousins have remained involved in each other's lives regardless of the miles between you. In this case, you may have a mutually beneficial relationship similar to that between Esther and Mordecai.

According to Esther 2:5–7, Mordecai loved his young cousin and had cared for her when she was orphaned. When she became the queen of Persia, Mordecai was glad for her success but did not take advantage of her position to gain favor for himself. For her part, Esther later demonstrated selfless love for Mordecai and her people by alerting her husband of a plot by his top advisor to exterminate the Jews—her extended family (chapters 4 and 5).

4–3. *How much would you sacrifice to help one of your cousins or your entire extended family? What does your answer indicate about the value you place on these relationships?*

Aunts And Uncles

Next to grandparents, your aunts and uncles are often your closest extended relationships, having grown up with your parents. But as with cousins and other relatives, such relationships are not always positive.

Take a moment to read Genesis 29:18–26. Jacob had pledged to work 7 years for his uncle in return for Laban's younger daughter Rachel. Imagine Jacob's surprise and anger when he lifted the veil of his new bride and discovered he had been married to Rachel's older sister Leah.

Laban's trick continued to reap pain for his daughters for years. Their relationships with Jacob were often strained, and even the joy of childbirth degenerated into a demeaning competition between these sister/wives.

Obviously, you will not have the same problems with your parents' siblings as Jacob had with Laban. But it may be that as an adult you now see the flaws in your aunts and uncles that were not apparent to you when you were a child. Parents, who can sometimes be blunt about the faults of their siblings, may try to involve you in issues between them and your aunts or uncles. It can be very easy to join in the critique, thankful you are part of the "good" branch of the family.

4–4.   *What, if any, negative things have you learned about your aunts and uncles? How has this information affected your relationships with them?*

4–5.   *In contrast, record as many positive things about each aunt or uncle as you can.*

Jacob and Laban's relationship worsened over the years, until Jacob finally took his family and left. The parting was so final that he and Laban set up markers to keep them forever separate (Genesis 31).

May your relationships with your aunts and uncles not have this end. Instead, may they reflect the positive aspects of relationships illustrated by Jehosheba and Paul's nephew.

4–6. *Read 2 Kings 11:2. How does Jehosheba's saving Joash illustrate a devoted relationship between an aunt and a nephew?*

The roles were switched in Acts 23:16–22. Paul's nephew risked his life to pass along news of a plot to kill his famous uncle. This young man demonstrated his devotion to his uncle by risking being discovered by those involved in the plot.

4–7. *What meaningful things could you do for your aunts and uncles that might demonstrate your love for them?*

Your aunts and uncles can give you more than stories of your parents as children. They can inspire and challenge you by the choices they make and the advice they give. While you will always be your parents' child, you can gain a valuable non-peer friendship by developing a close relationship with an aunt or uncle.

4–8.   *Select one aunt or uncle you would like to know better. What can you do this month to foster a closer relationship?*

In-Laws

As countless newlyweds have discovered, it is difficult to adjust to the traditions, habits, viewpoints, and personalities of one's in-laws—mother, father, sisters, and brothers. It is an adjustment, however, that is well worth making, both for peace in the home and the broadened perspective you can gain. Sadly, the number of in-law jokes you hear testifies about how many of us do not make the necessary adjustment.

4–9.   *What kind of a relationship do you have with your mother- and father-in-law?*

When in-law relationships are poor, they can be some of the worst possible. David saved his nation from military defeat and married King Saul's daughter. But his father-in-law's jealousy spawned a boundless hatred for him. According to 1 Samuel 18:12–29, Saul was willing to go to any length to see David dead. He even used his daughter's affection for David in an attempt to have him murdered (verses 20–27).

In contrast to Saul, Jethro was an excellent in-law. Exodus 18 shares an interesting account. Much of the journey from Egypt to Canaan lay ahead, and Moses was still the only commonly recognized authority in the huge camp. Jethro's advice to Moses was instrumental in establishing a chain of command to share leadership responsibilities.

4–10. What difficulties have you experienced in developing relationships with your in-laws?

4–11. What have you learned from the unique perspective and advice of your in-laws?

Relating to in-laws, and other mature relatives, can be a challenge. There are those who will try to manipulate the lives of those younger than them to their own advantage. Others, like Jethro, have much to offer and are able to do so in a manner that makes their advice something to be treasured. Godly relationships with in-laws are marked by an exchange of respect.

Chapter Review

Extended family relationships are important. The family unit as a whole is only as strong as its parts. God can help each member contribute to the loving commitment needed in families.

What can you do to contribute to the health of your extended family? First, keep in mind that you and your immediate family are not perfect. Most people tend to think their relatives, especially their in-laws, are the ones with the strange customs and annoying habits. But an honest look would make you confess that your ideas and preferences may seem just as peculiar to your relatives. Instead of joking about them behind their backs, learn to respect them as people and do what you can to build mutually beneficial relationships with each of them.

4–12. Record a prayer asking for God's help as you seek to improve your relationships with your extended family.

Part Two

Growing In Your Marriage

Society is utterly confused about what marriage is. Sadly, many Christian couples have replaced biblical standards with the world's shifting morals and conflicting values. These next chapters will help you to look at marriage in general—and yours in particular—through the lens of God's Word. Instead of taking your marriage and your spouse for granted, you can see in them the richness of God's blessings. And instead of attempting to work through troubles on your own, you can learn to cooperate with Him to make your marriage what He knows it can be.

You may think your marriage is beyond repair. Your spouse may be an unbeliever, or one of you may have been unfaithful. Even with these difficulties, God can help you rebuild—or build from scratch—a relationship of trust and godly love.

And if you are a single believer, you may learn some things that prepare you for marriage or help you understand better the struggles those who are married face.

Learning God's Marriage Design

With the divorce rate among church-goers reportedly equal to that among the general population, it seems many Christian husbands and wives do not know, or are not willing to accept, God's rules for marriage commitment and fidelity. People tend to want to make their own rules. The problem with this is that no human has the authority to change the rules God established.

What can you do to ensure that your marriage does not end up as part of a divorce rate statistic? God's Word is clear: you and your partner must choose to play by the rules. And you can learn about these rules in the Bible.

5–1. *From your own Bible reading and experience, what do you think God's design for marriage is?*

Knowing Marriage's Purpose

Considering why God established marriage will help you learn more about His plans for your marriage. To do this, you need to review the relationship between the first couple—Adam and Eve.

Read Genesis 2:18–23. Adam was made in God's image, but he was alone. His physical, intellectual, and spiritual nature cried out for companionship (verse 18). To fill this need, the Lord gave him Eve—a partner completely unlike anything else He created (verses 19–23).

5–2. *Why do you think God chose to create Adam and Eve this way instead of making them both at the same time?*

Obviously, God had a reason for creating Eve as He did. Some will say God was establishing male dominance by forming the woman from the man's rib. Verse 24, however, makes God's motivation clear: "For this reason a man will...be united to his wife, and they will become one flesh." Adam and Eve were created as more than mating partners: she was made from him, making them intimately and uniquely one (verse 23).

Marriage, then, is the physical and spiritual union of two into one. Many animals select mates for life, but only human spouses become "one flesh." When you married your spouse, you did more than agree to live with him or her for a lifetime:

you entered into a relationship that has as its end a oneness that cannot be experienced in any other way.

5–3. *If oneness is the purpose of marriage, why do you think the vast majority of married couples do not seem to experience it?*

Even among Christians, the idea of becoming "one flesh" rarely comes up before or after the wedding vows. Today's typical couples quickly get down to the business of living together as two individuals, forgetting that God intends for marriage to be a true union, not just a pairing. While it is important that you and your spouse understand yourselves individually, God's purpose for your marriage is that you be truly unified.

5–4. *Would you characterize your marriage as "one flesh" living in harmony or as two individuals cooperating? Explain your answer.*

5–5.   *What can you do this week to help there be more unity and less individualism between you and your spouse?*

Honoring Marriage's Permanence

When Adam and Eve committed the first sin, they were cast out of Eden. With sin came conflict—between God and them and between each other. Their descendants continued to marry, but the sanctity of their commitment to each other was dim in their eyes. Many sought union with people other than their husbands or wives. Many others opted to end their marriages. Even among the Jews, divorce became increasingly common.

By the time of Jesus' ministry, there were two schools of thought about divorce. In Deuteronomy 24:1, God allowed for divorce when a wife was found to be "indecent." The Jewish teacher Shammai taught that this referred to a gross act of indecency, such as adultery. In contrast, the teacher Hillel contended that anything displeasing—even a poor meal—was grounds for lawful divorce.

Some Pharisees, attempting to trick Jesus into taking one side on the controversial issue, confronted Him about divorce in Matthew 19:3–6. Jesus did not fall for the trap. Depending on Scripture rather than the teachings of Hillel or Shammai, Jesus made His point clear: Gods says that marriage is to be permanent.

5–6.   *Explain the reasoning Jesus used to declare that marriage should not be ended except through death.*

If marriage is two people becoming one, it follows that marriage was designed by God to be permanent, at least as long as both partners are alive. Jesus would allow for certain exceptions, but He first made it clear that marriage is not so cheap that it can be abandoned "for any and every reason" (verse 3). "No-fault divorce" was not in Jesus' vocabulary.

In almost every wedding today, vows of lifelong commitment are exchanged, only to be broken in far too many instances. Granted, there are circumstances in which even Jesus would allow divorce, but they cannot account for the extremely high rate of ended marriages in our society. It is clear that, as a Christian, you need to follow Jesus' standard even though it goes against what is believed and allowed in your culture.

5–7.   *What justifications have you heard others make concerning their divorces? How do these measure up to God's idea of marriage's permanence?*

5–8.   *Have you or another believer you know divorced over*
        what could be called less-than-Scriptural reasons? What
        do you think should be the response of other Christians?

Legalism must be avoided: Jesus never intended anything
He said to be made into a legalistic bully club. On the other
hand, you are not doing anyone good if you are so concerned
with a person's self-esteem that you refuse to point out when
he or she is wrong. It is difficult sometimes to balance
upholding biblical standards with acting with empathy and
compassion. Yet this is what must be done.

Appreciating Marriage's Sanctity

In Matthew 19:7–9, the Pharisees again attempted to
discredit Jesus by getting Him to say that Moses had been
wrong to command divorce. Jesus again responded in a way
that foiled their attempt by making a small, but important
distinction: Moses did not command divorce, but he did
permit it.

5–9.   *Why did the Law permit divorce if God is opposed to it?*

Jesus reaffirmed that allowing divorce was not a part of God's original intention for marriage. Then He echoed Shammai's teaching: divorce for any but the gravest reason is wrong (verse 9). Jesus' goal was not to define what made divorce allowable, but to raise His hearers' estimation of the sanctity of marriage.

5–10. *How does holding to strict standards for divorce affirm marriage's sanctity?*

Years after Jesus' confrontation with the Pharisees, the Corinthian believers found themselves entangled in several controversies over marriage relationships. In 1 Corinthians 7:10–14, Paul applied the principles Jesus established. The message is clear: preserve the marriage if at all possible. If your spouse is unsaved and is not committed to you, keep the marriage together for as long as possible to give that spouse time to respond to a steady witness. Whenever possible, the solution must be reconciliation, not dissolution.

5–11. *Have you or a friend been married to an unbeliever? How have you seen patient faithfulness with and a steady witness to one's unsaved spouse rewarded?*

Chapter Review

Listening to the family values rhetoric of today's politicians, you might think this culture is returning to biblical standards for marriage. But this is not the case. As long as men and women marry without a true understanding of what it means to be "one flesh," their marriages will not fulfill God's purpose and will be ill-equipped to resist the easy-out of divorce when conflicts arise.

5–12. **About which aspect of God's marriage design have you been more influenced by current trends and views? What can you do this month to help your marriage be more like God desires?**

Thankfully, you and your spouse have not been left to fend for yourselves in following God's design for your marriage. You have His help, as well as the counsel and example of other Christians. With daily effort and prayer, you and your spouse can experience the joy of becoming "one flesh."

With effort and God's help, a strong marriage can be built.

Building A Solid Relationship

What institution is joked about more than any other in modern culture? It is marriage. Stand-up comics base entire routines on jokes about marriage and all of its restrictions. Pastors make quips about it from the pulpit. Peers tease their friends who are about to be married about the loss of personal freedom and the onset of a life of drudgery. Yet almost without exception, these same people long for or seek to maintain the stability and love of a good marriage.

6–1. *What jokes have you heard that belittle the sanctity and blessing of marriage and promote attitudes harmful to the building of a firm marriage?*

Marriage does not have to be the prison so many jokingly call it. As you were reminded in the previous chapter, God's design for marriage has always been that it be good. Couples can unite and thrive in a quality marriage relationship. This chapter will remind you of some key characteristics that can help you build just such a solid relationship.

Committing To Be Faithful

One of the primary building blocks of a successful marriage is a firm commitment to fidelity. It is what you promised each other in your vows. Marriage is an exclusive, life contract—no exceptions allowed. Sadly, thousands destroy or greatly damage their marriages each year by forgetting—or ignoring—their vows to be faithful.

6–2.   *Do you know others whose marriages were ended by marital unfaithfulness? How has seeing their marriages destroyed by affairs affected your resolve to remain faithful to your spouse?*

According to Proverbs 5:15–19, sexual fulfillment with your spouse is an important deterrent against adultery. Many people seek affairs out of dissatisfaction with their married love life. The more content you are with the physical relationship you have with your spouse, the less likely it is that you will be tempted to be physically unfaithful.

6–3. *What is the danger of thinking that sexual fulfillment alone is enough to keep you faithful? What else is required?*

Verses like Hebrews 13:4 are straightforward reminders that sexual unfaithfulness has severe consequences. But these warnings cannot be your sole motivation for remaining true to your spouse. Faithfulness is a reflection of your character: Will you keep your promise to remain with your spouse for life? (See Matthew 19:4–6.) As you were reminded in the previous chapter, you and your spouse have become, in God's eyes, an inseparable unit.

6–4. *Write vows reaffirming your commitment to your spouse. Then arrange a romantic moment in which to share these vows with your spouse.*

Although some broken marriages are the result of one partner's unfaithfulness, many are broken by a simple lack of commitment. Jesus spoke very clearly: if God intends couples to stay together, faithfulness is a prerequisite for marriage.

Learning To Sacrifice

One thing the marriage jokes do get right is the amount of personal sacrifice that is required of you as a marriage partner. Both spouses must give up the pursuit of their own interests and desires in order to serve each other.

6–5.   What have you given up in order to better serve your spouse? How has this been a rewarding experience?

The premier Scripture passage on sacrifice in marriage is Ephesians 5:21–33. Many have misused this passage to teach a wife's subordination to her husband's lordship. Read properly, the verses call on both spouses to do what may be uncomfortable so they can better serve each other. Trusting submission (verse 22) and unsolicited nurturing (verse 25) are parallel: both actions require selflessness and sacrifice.

6–6.   Two of the primary needs of most women are security and comfort. How does this fact help to explain why it is difficult for many wives to yield to their husbands?

6–7. *Men are typically not good at listening or expressing love.*
       How might these characteristics be hurdles to a husband's
       acting in the Christlike way Ephesians 5:25–29 requires?

While Paul compared the husband's love for his wife to Christ's love for the Church, you must not take the analogy too far. Jesus can require complete obedience because He is infinitely wise and perfect: no husband can make that claim, nor can any wife expect it. In fact, if you look to your spouse to meet every need, you will be disappointed. Bolster your faith in the Lord's ability to meet your needs so you can concentrate on being a blessing to your spouse.

6–8. *Have you unrealistically expected your spouse to meet all*
       your needs? What needs and desires can you turn over to
       the Lord and allow Him to answer?

The world may see marriage as one of many means to gain personal fulfillment. As a believer, you can view the marital relationship as the best means to giving another fulfillment.

Fostering Intimacy

Within the bounds of faithfulness and self-sacrifice exists a great and wonderful intimacy unparalleled by any other closeness. If you and your spouse are believers, you are able to experience that intimacy as God originally designed it.

6–9. **How would you describe the emotional and spiritual intimacy you and your spouse share?**

Genesis 2:18–24 is again helpful in understanding God's marriage design. You and your spouse are to be more than cohabitating individuals: you are "one flesh." The intimacy the Lord wants you to have involves your complete person—spirit, soul, and body. You and your spouse are to be closest friends, as well as brothers and sisters in Christ. There are to be no secrets between you, creating a level of trust that is needed to maintain a healthy relationship.

6–10. **Would you describe your spouse as your best friend? What effect does this have on the intimacy in your marriage?**

In many ways, sexual intimacy is the keystone of a solid marriage. The apostle Paul, who recognized that practicalities are not unspiritual, advised married believers to enjoy their physical relationship unselfishly. According to 1 Corinthians 7:2–6, you and your spouse have a duty to one another because you have exchanged ownership, so to speak, of your bodies. A healthy sexual relationship will help you maintain purity by keeping both of you satisfied by each other.

6–11. How have you found that ongoing sexual intimacy has strengthened your non-sexual intimacy with your spouse?

Interestingly, Paul saw short periods of concentrated prayer as the only legitimate reason for abstaining from sex in marriage. In no way was he hinting that sexual intimacy is an unholy distraction for maturing believers. Like food to the body, sexual intimacy is necessary for the continued strength and vitality of a godly marriage.

6–12. What can you do this week to improve the intimacy between you and your spouse?

Chapter Review

You can enjoy a solid marriage with your spouse. Yet this kind of relationship is not easy: it will require a great amount of work. Self-sacrifice never comes easy; selfishness is much more in keeping with human nature. But a good marriage lasts for a lifetime, making it well worth the effort.

If you are married, examine your own attitudes about marriage and the actions that come out of them. Do not examine your spouse; the fastest way to hurt the marriage relationship is to look for faults in the other person. Determine to treasure the wonderful gift you have in your spouse. Every morning, recommit yourself to be faithful to him or her. Allow Christ to develop in you the character of selflessness necessary for a healthy marriage.

6–13. *Write a prayer you can offer daily that will ask the Lord to help you put your spouse before yourself.*

Making It Last

The story is told of an old beggar who lived on the streets and ate from garbage cans. His only possession was his "lucky rock" that he always carried in his pocket. One morning a police officer found the old beggar lying cold and stiff in an alley. When the authorities cataloged his only possession, someone noticed that his "lucky rock" was a valuable, uncut gem. The tragedy was that he had lived a life of poverty when in fact, he had unknowingly possessed great wealth.

Even more tragic is the situation in many of today's marriages. At the beginning of their life together, both spouses understood the gem they had in each other. Faithfulness was unquestioned, sacrifices for the sake of the other were made, and some level of intimacy was developed. But over time, the couple allowed the junk of living to accumulate on their relationships, until the once brilliant gem looks to them like the beggar's "lucky stone." This common progression accounts for the many divorces that occur after 10, 15, even 25 years of marriage.

As you read this chapter, examine your ongoing role in your marriage relationship. Are there areas in which you need to improve? Allow the Holy Spirit to reveal these areas and help you to change.

7–1. **What aspects of your being a godly spouse do you already know need improving? How has God helped you in the improvement process?**

Showing Consideration

God intends every marriage relationship to be one of mutual satisfaction and fulfillment. To accomplish this, you and your spouse must have consideration for each other. As you saw in the previous chapter, part of being considerate is meeting the sexual desires of your spouse (1 Corinthians 7:2 6). But it does not end there. Both of you must show consideration for the other's hopes, feelings, emotions, and individuality.

7–2. *Do you find it difficult to do things for your spouse that you do not want to do? How could you improve in this area?*

First Corinthians 7:32–35 is usually discussed only when addressing the Bible's views on singleness, but the passage contains some excellent observations about what is needed to maintain a healthy marriage. Again, the key is being willing to demonstrate loving concern for your spouse's happiness and well-being.

7–3. *Do you always consider the good of your spouse in every decision, including spiritual ones? How might doing this consistently change your marriage?*

Unless you continue to work at being more concerned about your spouse's happiness than your own, you and your spouse will gradually become less involved in each other's lives until each of you goes about his or her own business, interacting only when it is unavoidable. If you are, however, truly concerned about meeting the needs of your spouse, your marriage will maintain its vitality and strength.

7–4. *Ideally, both you and your spouse will look out for each others' interests. What are you to do if your spouse does not take this responsibility seriously?*

7–5.   *What three things could you start doing this week for your spouse that would show him or her that you are concerned about his or her needs and desires?*

Continuing To Honor

As with almost all couples, you and your spouse probably struggled early on to define your respective places. After a few months or years, you likely settled into a routine, each of you knowing what to expect from the other. Predictability is certainly comfortable, but it also puts your marriage at risk for a major danger—taking your spouse for granted.

7–6.   *Describe a time, past or present, when you found that you were taking your spouse for granted. What did you do to rejuvenate your respect and appreciation for him or her?*

Look again at Ephesians 5:21–28. If you want continued vitality in your relationship, keep on giving your husband or wife the honor and consideration God says he or she deserves. Paul grounded this mutual respect (expressed by mutual submission) in a "reverence for Christ" (verse 21). Honoring the Lord requires humility and recognition of your imperfections—attitudes that will also help you in honoring your spouse.

7–7.   How could you alert yourself if you were not submitting to—that is, showing proper respect for—your spouse?

Ephesians 5 is famous for the parallels it draws between husbands and wives and Christ and the Church. As was pointed out before, this is not to say that men have anywhere near the perfection of character and wisdom that Christ has. Submission is not for wives only: husbands have an equal responsibility. Wives must respect their husbands, just as husbands must respect their wives. The way this respect is expressed may differ, but its nature is the same—recognition and appreciation of each other's value.

7–8.   List five traits of your spouse that you admire. (If you find this difficult to do, pray for God to open your eyes and record the traits as you notice them over several days.)
   •
   •
   •
   •
   •

Peter also elaborated on the need for mutual respect in marriage. According to 1 Peter 3:1–6, a wife's true beauty is seen in the way she honors her husband unconditionally.

7–9.   *How would you describe the character and personality of a wife with godly beauty? (If you are a wife, ask God to develop these traits in you.)*

A husband's attitude is no less important. First Peter 3:6 makes it clear that a godly husband treats his wife with respect and kindness, being unconditionally considerate of her feelings and needs.

7–10. *What would a genuinely considerate husband do? (If you are a husband, ask God to develop these habits in you.)*

Many couples—even Christians—have divorced because mutual respect was either never developed or lost over time. To preserve the health of your marriage, consciously remember how privileged you are to be married to your spouse.

Loving Like Christ Loves

Genuine, caring love is, by far, the most important ingredient in a healthy marriage. And there is always hope. Many couples have rejuvenated their marriages by remembering why they fell in love in the first place.

7–11. What attracted you to each other? Why did you marry?

But stirring up the old romance will not provide the enduring love your marriage needs. You can learn this love by watching and talking with older married couples. Yet the best pattern for real love is Jesus Christ. As Ephesians 5:25 instructs, you are to love your husband or wife with the same depth and intensity that Christ demonstrated on the cross.

7–12. What can you do to develop, revive, or maintain Christ's kind of love for your wife or husband?

Chapter Review

With marriage taken so lightly by today's society, it is not surprising that a healthy, long-term relationship seems to demand more effort now that it ever has. Whether this is fact or perception, the Bible stills provides the best advice for keeping your marriage happy and productive for years to come. Of course, it is up to you to apply that advice to the relationship between you and your spouse.

7–13. **Having looked at the need for ongoing consideration, respect, and love, what strikes you as the area in which you are doing the best? What area could use the most improvement?**

Remember that God desires you to have the best marriage possible. He will help you make the necessary changes to improve and strengthen your relationship. Ask Him to help you to be the best marriage partner you can be.

Living Unequally Yoked

8–1. *When you married, were you and your husband or wife Christians? What about now? Describe your spouse's relationship with the Lord.*

The past three chapters on a godly marriage were based on a very important assumption—that both you and your spouse are devoted believers. But sadly, this is not always the case. You may have received Christ after marriage. You may have married an unbeliever. Or your spouse may have strayed from the Lord since you married. Whatever the details are, if you are married to an unbeliever, you may find help and hope in this chapter. If you are married to a Christian, these pages may prepare you to help a Christian friend who is married to an unbeliever or considering such a marriage.

Recognizing The Danger

Before looking at ways you, or someone you know, can deal with being married to an unbeliever, it is vital that you see what God has to say about such relationships and what the likely pitfalls are. This preventive medicine can be of benefit if you or someone you know is contemplating marrying one who is not a Christian.

8–2.   **Read 2 Corinthians 6:14 through 7:1. What do you think it means to be "yoked together"?**

Like oxen or horses joined to pull a load, you and your spouse need to move together in the same direction. Paul made it clear: a believer and an unbeliever are headed in opposite directions.

8–3.   **How do you think so many Christians can justify dating unbelievers, let alone marrying them?**

Some Christians pursue relationships with unbelievers in the blind hope that they may be saved. But for those who "missionary date," the relationship often becomes more important than their commitment to Christ. Then the believer either abandons his or her faith or enters a marriage doomed for conflict. For every rare "success" story, there are many others that end in misery.

8–4. *Have you or someone you know had a serious relationship with an unbeliever? What were the consequences?*

No matter how important a relationship might seem, it cannot take priority over the health of your relationship with the Lord. As hard as it might be to break off a relationship with an unbeliever now, honestly evaluate your future with that person. If marriage were to result, you would have to choose between holding to your faith in spite of your spouse's disapproval or wholeheartedly giving yourself to him or her at the expense of your relationship to the Lord. Now is the time to make the right choice.

Learning From Others

King Solomon's life is the perfect illustration of what Paul warned against: having a close relationship with an unbeliever. Solomon started off well—the favorite son of the legendary King David, the wisest man in history, a ruler with staggering wealth and world-wide fame (1 Kings 3:3–14; 10:23–25). Because of his initial obedience to the Lord, Solomon was blessed as few others are.

But Solomon's weakness for women led him to marry pagan wives whose influence drew the once-wise king into blatant idolatry. Reading 1 Kings 11:1–13 is sobering. The righteous king famous for building the temple to the Lord became the compromised old man who had temples built for a myriad foreign idols and incurred God's anger (verse 9). Only the Lord's promise to Solomon's father would keep at least a portion of the kingdom in the family (verse 13).

8–5. *Solomon was the wisest person ever, yet he compromised God's law because of his wives. How does this illustrate the negative influence an unbelieving spouse can have?*

Solomon's sad example still speaks powerfully today. No one can sustain a relationship in which Jesus Christ is not the center and expect to remain close to the Lord. It is vital that both marriage partners agree in their commitment to God.

Dealing With An Unsaved Spouse

All this advice is very important, but what if you are already the spouse of someone unsaved? If this is your case—because you married despite the warnings or became a Christian after your were married—how are you to handle it?

First, you must seek and accept the Lord's forgiveness. If you knowingly married an unbeliever as a Christian, you may be haunted by a sense of God's displeasure. Although God is not pleased when His children marry an unbeliever, He has not condemned or abandoned you. If you ask His forgiveness, He will give it, along with whatever else you need to live for Him in your marriage.

8–6. *Why would Christians who married unsaved people have difficulty feeling they have been forgiven? What would you tell someone in this situation that could help him or her seek and truly accept God's forgiveness?*

Second, you must stick with it. You have a responsibility to the Lord to remain in the marriage, using any opportunity you find to point your partner to Christ. Although it was not God's will for you to marry a non-Christian, it is His will now that you make the marriage the best you can.

8–7. *If your spouse does not turn to the Lord despite your best efforts, what can you do to be spiritually and emotionally fulfilled?*

Third, you must make the Lord first in your life regardless of whether your spouse does. You will not be deprived in your relationships if you develop your relationship with God.

A dynamic faith is an absolute must. If your relationship with God is half-hearted and does not affect your character, then your unsaved spouse will want to have nothing to do with the Lord. But if He is everything to you and you allow Him to be seen in your words and actions, your spouse will take interest.

8–8.   *What can you do to help yourself pursue your relationship with God without making your unsaved spouse feel shut out of that area of your life?*

This brings up the fourth response to having an unbelieving spouse: you must entrust his or her spiritual condition to God. Let the Lord bring conviction. You cannot save your spouse, nor does God expect you to.

8–9.   *Have you or someone you know pushed too hard trying to get a spouse to accept Christ? What was the result? What can you learn from the situation?*

Two passages—1 Corinthians 7:12–16 and 1 Peter 3:1,2—will help you have a balanced perspective. While you are to do your best to live a Christian life before your unsaved spouse, he or she—not you—is ultimately responsible for his or her eternal destiny. If your spouse accepts Christ because of your life witness, praise the Lord! But if not, you must realize that God allows people to make their own choices.

8–10. *What role do you think prayer can play in a marriage between a believer and a non-Christian, both for the praying spouse and the one being prayed for?*

Chapter Review

Looking again at Solomon, it is interesting to wonder what his life would have been like if he had committed himself to only one God-fearing woman in marriage. Almost without doubt, Solomon's initial fervor for the Lord would have remained throughout his life.

Prevention is the best safeguard you have against being trapped as Solomon was. If you are looking for a relationship, do not even consider being involved with a non-Christian. Even if it appears to start innocently as just a "date," you must be careful. The best course is to avoid the pitfall altogether by filling your social and spiritual life with other committed Christians.

8–11. *Think of a Christian friend or family member who is in a relationship with an unsaved person. From the principles you have learned in this chapter, what could you share with him or her that might make a difference?*

Of course, you may already be married to an unbeliever. You can still thrive as a Christian in such a way that your spouse is attracted to what you have. And you can live with peace knowing that God will use your daily witness to draw your husband or wife's heart toward himself.

And if you are married to a wonderful Christian, you can be an encouragement to those with unsaved spouses. They need your empathetic ear and prayer-bathed advice. It may be that you will be able one day to hear a friend testify about his or her spouse's salvation.

Overcoming Adultery

Even in this immoral society, the word *adultery* stirs strong, negative emotions. Those who accept casual sex and no-fault divorce still react negatively to adultery. Being unfaithful is almost universally recognized as wrong and shameful.

9–1. *How would you react if you learned that a friend or family member had committed adultery?*

Unfortunately, Christians are not automatically sheltered from adultery. Many believers have lost their marriages because their spouses were unfaithful. Even David—"man after [God's] own heart" (1 Samuel 13:14)—angered God with his adultery and attempts to hide it (2 Samuel 11:27).

Guarding Against Temptation

If you strive to live faithfully for God and with your spouse, you will not likely set yourself up for moral failure. Adultery, however, usually results from the subtle, seemingly harmless choices you make. When your guard against these temptations is dropped, you are open to sin and eventual defeat.

9–2.   How have you been tempted to be unfaithful to your spouse? If you resisted, how did you do it?

Ironically, moral failure can occur during times of success. According to 2 Samuel 11:1, King David was enjoying palace ease while his army made war without him. Life was good. Nothing, it seemed, could go wrong. Worse, it is apparent David thought nothing he might do could be wrong. Overconfident and lazy, his attitude led him past temptation to blatant sin (verses 2–5).

9–3.   How might David have handled temptation if he had been personally and spiritually disciplined?

If your marriage has settled into a rut and your relationship with the Lord is dry, you are a prime target for temptation. It is when you are taking your marriage for granted that you are more likely to take a second look at that person in the office, at church, or at the grocery store.

9–4. **What two things can you do this week to revitalize your relationships with God and your spouse?**

The rest of 2 Samuel 11 illustrates the danger of yielding to temptation. Having lusted from the roof, sending for another man's wife seemed a natural second step (verse 4). Being alone with her quickly led to sinning sexually with her. Learning Bathsheba was pregnant, David's first thought was to get her husband home from the war to make it seem the child was his (verses 6–13). When this failed, it was not a big a step for David to order Uriah killed in a military skirmish (verses 14–26).

9–5. **Have you seen others fall into adultery after making "minor mistakes"? How did things progress to sexual immorality?**

The story of David and Bathsheba reveals immorality's deceptive power. You may think you can draw the line later. But according to James 1:14,15, unchecked desire always leads to sin, which naturally ends in death. Deal with sin at the first temptation. Douse any interest in someone besides your spouse the minute you are aware of it.

Reaping God's Judgment

David tried to act as if everything were normal until God's prophet confronted him about his affair (2 Samuel 12:1–7). Nathan's parable excited David's indignation, then exposed him for the adulterer he was. His sins had found him out.

9–6. *Do you think God exposes every adultery? Does anyone ever really "get away" with committing adultery?*

Hebrews 13:4 warns that "God will judge the adulterer and all the sexually immoral." Adultery, whether one-time or ongoing, yields devastating and inevitable consequences.

9–7. *Is there a difference between the natural consequences of a sin and God's judgment? Why or why not?*

God's judgment would hound David (verses 8–14). The child conceived in adultery would die. He would be betrayed by someone close. And violence would plague his family.

9–8.   What additional consequences of their affair do you think David and Bathsheba faced?

Had David realized beforehand the consequences of his actions, it is doubtful he would have done what he did. Lust and power blinded him into thinking he would get away with it.

Your spouse may never find out about an affair, but you can be sure you will have to live with the unpleasant consequences. Even with forgiveness, the direct and indirect results remain.

9–9.   With so much to lose as a result of their sin, why do you think some people still choose to commit adultery?

If you have committed adultery and seem to have escaped detection, do not think God is not concerned about your sin. In His mercy, He has given you opportunity to confess and repent. Take advantage of that opportunity so the full weight of His judgment does not fall on you and your family.

9–10. *If you have been unfaithful, outline a confession you can use to seek your spouse's forgiveness. If you are faithful, write a prayer asking God to help you to remain faithful.*

You are not immune to adultery's allure or consequences. Many families, with husbands and wives just like you, have been destroyed by it. The greatest tragedy, however, is not the sufferings in this life but the prospect of eternal hell. First Corinthians 6:9,10 makes it clear that there is no hope of heaven for the unrepentant adulterer.

Finding Forgiveness

As you have seen, God judges sin. He also forgives and restores. When David finally confessed his wickedness, God's forgiveness was guaranteed immediately (2 Samuel 12:13).

9–11. *What can you learn about God's willingness to forgive from His immediate forgiveness of David?*

God's instant forgiveness of David can be a difficult thing to accept. Although David still suffered the consequences and judgments for his adultery, he was forgiven.

9–12. *Read Psalm 51. How important is it that David recognized both his wickedness and his unworthiness to be forgiven?*

If you or your spouse has been unfaithful, forgiving is a major issue. It is one of the most difficult things a husband or wife can do—so much so that it can be done only with God's help.

9–13. *If your spouse has been unfaithful, how can you allow the Lord to help your forgive him or her? If you have been unfaithful, what can you do to reaffirm your love and rebuild your spouse's trust?*

Rebuilding a healthy marriage after adultery is extremely difficult for both spouses, but it is possible. The restoration will almost certainly take months or even years. But if both the wronged spouse and the one who was unfaithful are fully committed to seeing their marriage restored, God will give them the strength and patience they need.

Chapter Review

The account of David and Bathsheba is tragic. But out of that tragedy shines a beam of hope: God forgives when the adulterer repents. An affair does not have to be the end of a marriage—yours or anyone else's. With the Lord's help, you and your spouse can overcome adultery.

Better yet, with the Lord's help, you can avoid adultery altogether. Take preventative measures: be alert to temptation, remain close to the Lord, and concentrate on nurturing the Christ-centered relationship between you and your spouse as chapters 6 and 7 showed you.

9–14. What have you learned from this chapter that will most help you affair-proof your marriage?

Part Three

Raising Godly Children

Parenting is a great challenge in today's society. Your children are very likely learning values and ideas from their friends and classmates that are contrary to the Bible. Entertainment is increasingly vulgar. But you are not alone in trying to raise godly children. As a Christian parent, you can have God's help, giving you more wisdom, patience, and sensitivity than you would have on your own.

The Bible makes it clear you are responsible for teaching your children about God and handing down biblical values. Do not depend on Sunday School teachers and other church leaders to give your children a spiritual education. Use a variety of methods—modeling, prayer, and family devotions—to instill godly ways of thinking and acting.

You do not have to be a Bible scholar or educational expert to raise godly children. And you will make mistakes. But love and sincerity will help both you and your children get through and learn from the tough times.

Accepting Parental Responsibilities

Do you remember when you found out you were going to be a parent? You had heard raising a child was work, but you could not imagine what all the fuss was about. Then reality hit.

Three a.m. feedings. Endless diapers. Toddler-proofing the cabinets. Picking up the house—again. Making lunches. Attending school plays. Coaching soccer. And that is just the work. You also have the big picture to think about—your child's physical, emotional, social, and spiritual development.

You may have so many things happening that you feel as if being a good parent is impossible. This chapter will help you transform that overwhelming to-do list into a few, basic responsibilities that the Lord has given to all believing parents.

Teaching About God

Just before the Israelites entered Canaan, Moses reviewed the Law with them a final time. To have God's blessing, they would need to diligently obey His commands (Deuteronomy 6:1–3). To do this, they had to honor God as first (verses 4,5) and pass down their faith to their children (verses 7–9).

10–1. *Who was made responsible for passing God's commands to the next generation? Why do you think this was so?*

Sunday School, children's church, and the youth group can play only limited roles in your children's spiritual education. The full responsibility for teaching them about God is yours.

Deuteronomy 6:7 speaks of relational teaching. Infuse your daily conversations with tidbits about who God is, how He works, and the kind of persons He wants your children to be. Whenever possible, encourage your children's spiritual curiosity, helping them discover the things of God.

10–2. *What are some common situations and times in which casual discussions with your children about serving God might be started naturally?*

Obviously, relational teaching requires that you have close relationships with your children. If you do not have such relationships, pray for God's help in strengthening the ties between you and your children.

10–3. Deuteronomy 6:8,9 speaks of visible symbols of the faith. How might these help a child learn about the Lord?

Orthodox Jews take these verses literally, going so far as to wear phylacteries (little boxes with Scripture written on parchment inside) on their foreheads and forearms when they pray. But you do not have to do this or write verses on every door frame of your house to follow God's instructions. The idea is that you surround your children with tangible reminders of the faith, share everyday object lessons, and start spiritual discussions by pointing out religious symbols in your home and around the community.

10–4. What are some simple things you could place around the house to help you pass on your faith to your children?

Of course, the most direct way to teach your children about the Lord is to read the Bible with them and lead them in prayer. Devotional times are vital in your children's spiritual education. You will read more about them in chapter 11.

10–5. *What specific things about knowing and serving God do you want your children to learn?*

Employing Godly Discipline

Part of teaching a child is providing consistent discipline. Even the most well-mannered, respectful child will disobey: it is a fact of the fallen human nature. Although it is the rare parent who wants to correct his or her children, doing so is a necessary part of training for life. The child who does not learn obedience and respect at home will become an adult who suffers because of his or her foolish rebellion.

10–6. *How have you seen someone who was not disciplined at home grow up to be an uncontrolled adult?*

First Samuel tells a tragic story that illustrates what can happen when a parent refuses to discipline his or her children. The high priest Eli was a godly man, but his sons were not.

Unsupervised, the young men treated the sacrifices with contempt (2:12–17) and slept with women who served at the tabernacle (verse 22). When their vile acts were reported to Eli, he made only weak attempts at correcting them (see verses 22–25). The result was disastrous and irreversible: both sons would die, the rest of the family would be plagued with short lives, and the priesthood would pass to another family (2:29–36; 3:11–14).

10–7. *According to 1 Samuel 2:29, Eli showed that he honored his sons more than God by not disciplining them. Is this true of all parents who do not discipline? Why or why not?*

The Book of Proverbs contains sound advice concerning disciplining children. Punishment for wrongdoing is needed at times (13:24). Of course, physical discipline is never an excuse for physical abuse. The key is being consistent with the reason for and method of discipline.

10–8. *When and to what degree do you think physical discipline is necessary? When and to what degree is it excessive?*

Proverbs 19:18 urges you to discipline your children before it is too late. If you indulge your children by not disciplining them, they may grow up to be disciplined by the law or destroyed by sinful lifestyles.

10–9. How does external discipline by parents transform into internal discipline—a child's self-control?

Another aspect of discipline is godly training—that is, helping your children develop spiritual disciplines. Proverbs 22:6 is the famous verse on the subject. While it is generally true that children raised in godly homes are more likely to serve the Lord as adults than children from ungodly homes, this verse is not a guarantee that your children will grow up to be solid Christians. Spiritual training can greatly shape your children, but it can never force them to live for God.

10–10. What can you do to help make sure your children's spiritual disciplines are truly theirs and not your own?

10–11. How would you encourage a Christian parent whose son or daughter has turned from the Lord?

One of the best ways to guard against your children's rebelling against your discipline is to make sure you always do it with love and consistency. Disciplining out of frustration or anger does no good; worse, it may give your children reason to resent you (Ephesians 6:4).

Disciplining is not enjoyable, but its benefits far outweigh its difficulty. If you always keep in mind that discipline is the means to a end—obedient, self-controlled children—instead of an end in itself, both you and your children will eventually see your disciplining them as a priceless gift.

Demonstrating Love

Above all, you have a responsibility to show your children genuine love. Even if they do not listen to your instructions or respond to discipline, you are still responsible to give them unconditional love. This is demonstrated clearly in the Parable of the Prodigal Son (Luke 15). The father did not make excuses for his son's behavior, but waited for and readily forgave him when he returned.

You do not have to wait for your children to rebel before you show love. And that is the key: your love must be shown, not just spoken. You can demonstrate genuine care for and devotion to your children in a thousand ways.

10–12. What five things could you do this week that would show
       your children how much you love them?

-
-
-
-
-

Your children need regular time and attention more than
gifts or big events. Their fondest memories of you will not be
what you gave them but the shoulder-rides, the bedtime
prayers, the lunchbox notes, and the porch-swing chats.

Chapter Review

Parenting is an enormous responsibility—one for which you
may feel inadequate at times. But be encouraged. God gave
you this task, and He will help you to complete it. You can
teach your children about the things of God by depending on
His Spirit for what to say and when to say it. You can discipline
well by using the wisdom God gives you. And you can give
your children the unconditional love they need by allowing the
Lord to love through you at all times.

10–13. You will be a better parent if you personally are teachable,
       disciplined, and loving. On what area would you like to
       work this week? What can you do to improve in this area?

Leading Family Devotions

As a parent who wants God's best for your children, you must take the reins of their spiritual education. One way to do this is to establish a regular time together with God that is relevant and enjoyable for both you and your children. This chapter will review the purpose of family devotions, spark your devotional creativity, and remind you again of the impact family devotions can have on your children.

11–1. *Relate your experiences with family devotions, both as a child and as an adult.*

Teaching Your Children The Faith

It has been said that religious movements tend to stagnate by the third generation unless deliberate care is taken to keep the faith fresh and hand it down intact. Read Deuteronomy 4:9,10. Personal study of biblical principles helps you not "let them slip from your heart"; family devotions help you "teach them to your children."

11–2. How can family devotions help you to hand down your faith to your children?

The same idea is restated in Deuteronomy 6:6,7. Note again the two-pronged emphasis: "These commandments... are to be upon *your hearts*. Impress them on *your children*" (emphasis added).

11–3. Is it vital that a parent have personal devotions in addition to family devotions? Why or why not?

According to Psalm 78:1–8, teaching your children about the Lord establishes an ongoing cycle of handing down the faith. It also safeguards them from repeating the mistakes of past generations. Whether discussing biblical accounts of Israel with you or hearing events from your own walk with God, your children will learn from the experiences of others. Ideally, deliberate teaching through family devotions will give your children a more mature faith than even you had.

11–4. In what ways would you like your children to have better understandings of God and His ways than you have?

11–5. Psalm 78:9–72 outlines Israel's spiritual victories and failures. What milestones and pitfalls in your spiritual walk could you share with your children during family devotions?

When you lead family devotions, you are fulfilling the mandate of Ephesians 6:4: "Bring [your children] up in the training and instruction of the Lord." These times together help your children form and practice godly skills and habits, as well as learn biblical rules and principles for daily living.

Tailoring Devotions To Your Children

You may be wondering, *Now that I know how vital family devotions are to my children's spiritual development, how should I go about leading them? Do I simply read a Bible chapter to my children then have them pray? Are there more creative means of passing the faith along?*

There is really no perfect method for leading family devotions. A myriad factors will affect when and how you hold these family times with God—your children's ages, their interests, their personalities, and their attention spans; your familiarity with Scripture and its principles; the family schedule; and so on.

11–6. List facts about your children that could affect the way you conduct devotions with your family?

Several guidelines can help you tailor devotions to your family. First, keep your children's attention by interacting on their developmental level. Use a Bible translation your children can understand. Keep your words simple. Share illustrations from their world. Reinforce what you are teaching with projects and object lessons. The more your children are involved, the better they will learn.

11–7. How does Deuteronomy 6:8,9 affirm the need for a multi-sensory approach to teaching your children the faith?

Second, consciously establish spiritual memories and reminders. When Israel crossed the Jordan River into Canaan, the Lord gave Joshua a creative way for the Israelites to teach their children. According to Joshua 4:4–7, a pile of rocks from the river was erected to help Israelite parents pass on their godly heritage.

11–8. What spiritual milestones in your children's lives would you like to commemorate? What are several creative ways you might help them remember one such event?

Third, make maximum use of the family devotion resources that are available: children's Bibles, devotional books, activity guides, animated and live-action videos, and children's ministry manuals. You can either center your family devotions on one resource at a time or create your own "curriculum" of sorts by selecting components from several resources. While doing this will require more preparation time and cost more than simply reading a chapter from the Bible, your children are likely to learn better with a creative approach.

11–9. *What family devotion resources do you already own, can be borrowed from your church, or could be purchased at a reasonable cost? (Do a little research and add items to this list as you find them.)*

Fifth, establish a regular time for your family devotions in addition to the unscheduled discussions you have with your children about the Lord (Deuteronomy 6:7). Some possibilities are at breakfast, after supper, and at bedtime. Availability and convenience are important considerations, but you may have to eliminate or reschedule other activities to make room. Consider family times with God one of your higher priorities.

11–10. *Why do you think it is so important that family devotions be regularly scheduled? How would you handle unavoidable time conflicts?*

Sixth, allow your children to have input into the structure and content of family devotions. Joshua's pillar of river stones, for instance, was intended to spark children's curiosity and help them initiate a teaching opportunity with a question (Joshua 4:6). Since the point of family devotions is to pass the faith on to your children, their sense of ownership is crucial.

11–11. *If your children came up with the plan for family devotions, what would they be like? What can you learn from this that will help you develop devotions that best impact them?*

Shaping Your Children's Lives

11–12. *What would you like to see your children gain from regular, family devotions while they are growing up?*

Will the effort of leading family devotions really make a difference in the lives of your children? Almost certainly.

Using Proverbs 22:6 again, the word translated "train" expresses the idea of directing the growth of a plant by bending, pruning, and tying. Family devotions are one of the ways you can encourage the spiritual growth of your children in the proper direction. The child who grows up viewing prayer, worship, and Bible study as a normal part of life is well on his or her way to serving the Lord faithfully.

Chapter Review

With so much to do each day, making time for family devotions may seem like too much trouble. Think for a moment, however, about the spiritual returns you can receive later from investments you make in your children today. In the moments you spend together as a family, communing with God through prayer and His Word, you mold character for a lifetime and plant in your children a hunger for God.

Instilling Godly Character

It has always been important that Christian parents raise children to hold to biblical values, but that importance is magnified when your children live in a world that denies even the most basic values. Even dependability and loyalty—two characteristics that were once assumed by most people—are rarely found in most children. As you teach your children about the Lord, the Bible, and spiritual disciplines, do not forget to consciously instill in them the character traits every godly person should possess.

This chapter is by no means an exhaustive treatment of godly values. It will, however, give you a starting place in helping your children exhibit good character.

Accountability

Accountability—the willingness to accept responsibility or to account for your actions—is the building block of all other godly character traits. Unless your children understand they are accountable to you, others, and God, they will not likely care about other issues of character.

You do not want your children to think God eagerly waits for a mistake to be made so He can punish them. But it is important for your children to realize they are primarily accountable to God. Others, including you, may not know all your children's thoughts or actions, but God sees everything.

12–1. *What do Matthew 12:36; 1 Corinthians 4:5; and 2 Corinthians 5:10 teach about your children's accountability to God?*

Your children also need to understand they are accountable to everyone, not just God and those who have authority over them. The apostle Paul demonstrated this fact in 2 Corinthians 8:16–23.

12–2. *Why do you think Paul, who founded Corinth's church and had authority there, felt it necessary to send three known leaders to collect the special offering from that church?*

If your children are going to practice the kind of above-and-beyond accountability demonstrated by Paul, they need to learn to do it early in life. With accountability a rarely practiced character trait in today's society, your example and influence are immeasurably important.

12–3. In what ways do you model a positive attitude about being accountable to God? to leaders? to your children? How well is this attitude communicated?

Respect

For your children to truly see themselves as accountable to others, they must genuinely respect them. Your children may be smarter or faster or funnier than others, but they are certainly not more important than others in God's eyes.

In 1 Timothy 5:1–4, Paul taught the young pastor the proper way to treat members of his congregation. Those older than Timothy were to be exhorted, not rebuked. Younger men were to appreciated. Women were to be honored. Widows were to be recognized and helped. Always, the rule was to show respect, regardless of a person's standing.

12–4. What traditions of respect for your elders and those in authority were you taught as a child?

12–5. *In what ways could you teach your children to have genuine respect for both superiors and peers?*

Loyalty

Another key component of godly values is loyalty. Lack of loyalty is an obvious show of disrespect and unaccountability. If your children honor and are accountable to the Lord, they will remain true to Him. Similarly, your children will be faithful to those they respect.

The story of David and Jonathan is a superb example of loyalty. Jonathan's father, King Saul, wanted to kill David out of jealousy for his throne. Even though it seems Jonathan knew that David would be the next king instead of him, the prince still protected his friend's life at the risk of his own. First Samuel 20:11–17 records David and Jonathan's pact of loyalty with each other and each other's families.

12–6. *Jonathan was more loyal to David than to his own father. How does a person of character determine where the greater loyalty ought to be?*

Loyalty can be expressed in several ways. Your children need to learn the importance of keeping promises, staying with someone through difficulty, not betraying confidences, and not rejecting others when they fail. Once again, your example is as vital as your instructions.

12–7. *What are your children learning from you about loyalty? How can you be a better example of what a loyal friend is?*

Honesty

One of the most obvious signs of a child's godly character is his or her consistent honesty. In contrast to the modern attempt to define a lot of gray areas, the Bible is black and white about honesty: "It is impossible for God to lie" (Hebrews 6:18), but Satan "is a liar and the father of lies" (John 8:44). Teach your children to follow God's example by being as honest as possible.

12–8. *How do you usually deal with your children's dishonesty? What do you do to encourage them to tell the truth?*

Sadly, many children learn the art of telling "white" lies from their parents. Listen to yourself carefully as you go through a day. Do you slander, bend or stretch the truth, intentionally mislead, hide important information, or say things you do not mean just to be polite? Your children are learning from you.

12–9. According to Deuteronomy 25:13–16, God "detests" deceit for personal gain. How are the examples of "white" lies listed above selfish and displeasing to God?

12–10. In what areas do you need to improve your own honesty so you can be a role model for your children?

Dependability

One of the best affirmations of your children's character will come when they are persons on whom God and others can depend. This is not to say your children will be perfect.

An illustration of the importance of dependability is found in 2 Kings 12:4–15. When King Joash found that the priests were using funds designated for temple repairs to pay for daily operations, he turned the responsibility over to people he trusted. These supervisors were so dependable that Joash knew he could trust them completely (verse 15).

12–11. How dependable would you say your children are? By what things do you measure your children's dependability?

In Luke 19, Jesus told the familiar Parable of the Talents. Although this parable speaks of God's ultimate judgment of how we used what He has given us, it can also teach your children valuable principles about dependability. The dependable are entrusted with greater responsibilities (verses 16–19), but those who cannot be relied on are punished for their lack of character (verses 20–24).

12–12. What tasks can you give your children to begin teaching them to be dependable?

Chapter Review

Accountability, respect, loyalty, honesty, and dependability are all character traits your children need to develop. God has given you, as a Christian parent, the responsibility to raise your children for Him. Seek His guidance in developing the character and values of your children.

12–13. What additional character traits and godly values do you hope to instill in your children?

As you have been regularly reminded in this chapter, the best way you can instill godly values in your children is to model them yourself. Pray daily that God will enable you to be the example of character your children need.

Notes

Notes

Notes

Notes